A Light in the

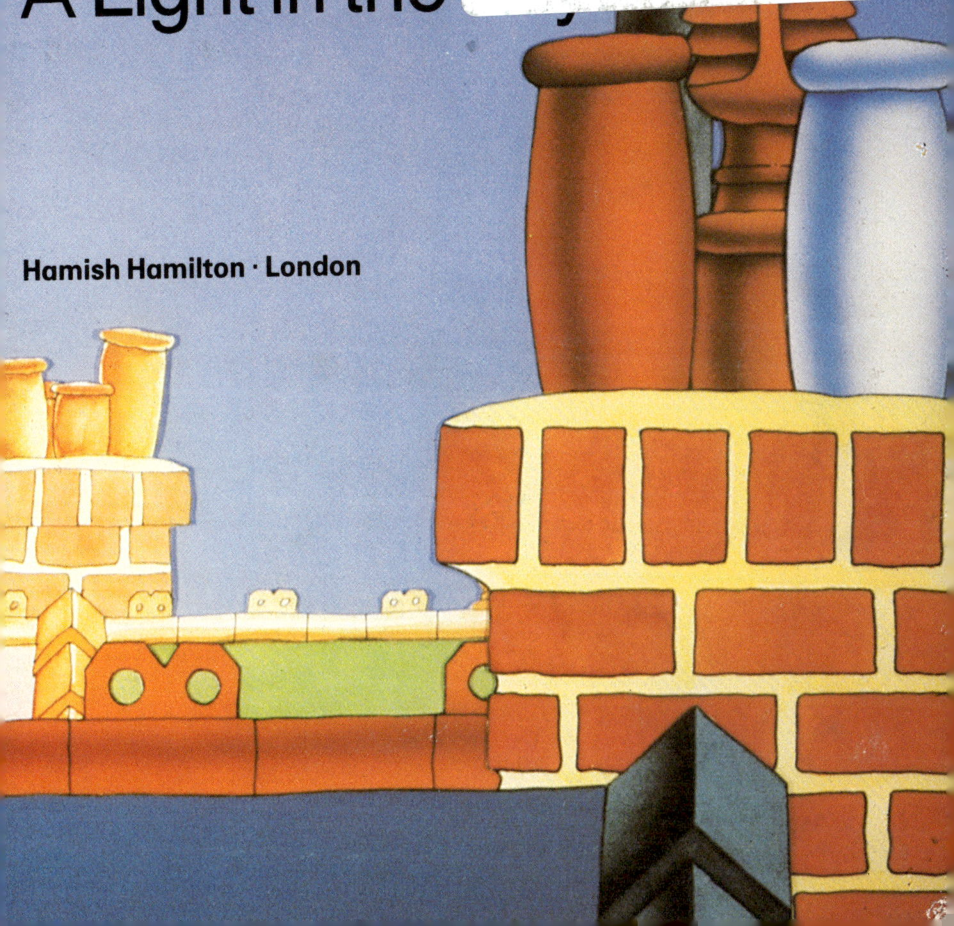

Hamish Hamilton · London

First Published in Great Britain 1982 by
Hamish Hamilton Children's Books
Garden House, 57–59 Long Acre, London WC2E 9JZ

British Library Cataloguing in Publication Data
Cole, Michael
Light in the sky.—(A Pigeon Street book)
I. Title II. Rogers, Alan
823'.914[J] PZ7
ISBN 0 241 10729 6

Phototypeset by Tradespools Limited, Frome, Somerset
Printed in Great Britain by
W.S. Cowell Ltd.
Butter Market, Ipswich

Written by Michael Cole
Illustrated by Alan Rogers
Photography by Peter Lang
Stories from the BBC TV series *Pigeon Street*
produced by David Yates Limited

It is autumn, and the leaves are falling. Molly and Polly try to catch a leaf on its way down, but whenever they reach out for it, the wind blows it on.

Reg the sweeper has plenty to do today. There are lots of fallen leaves to sweep up. While he works, he thinks of going dancing in the evening with his wife Doreen.

Mr Baskerville is on the green with his dog Watson. Mr Baskerville likes looking down at things through his magnifying glass. He can see a ladybird very clearly.

Mr Jupiter is on the green too with his dog Flash. He likes looking up at the sky through his telescope. The moon is already bright. It gets dark earlier now.

But something else is shining in the sky, Reg spots it. Then it moves. "Is it a spark from my bonfire?" he wonders.

Then Mr Jupiter spots it "Ah Gerald," he says "The first star is out. Look!" But when Gerald goes to look, the light moves. "Odd, most odd," says Mr Jupiter.

Hugo sees the light move. "I must be seeing things," he says. "Can it be something I've eaten?" But Clara has seen it too, driving her lorry home down the motorway.

P

Everybody in Pigeon Street is out wondering what the light can be. "It's an unidentified flying object, William," says Dr Glossop, and photographs it.

Mr Baskerville is looking through the telescope when the light disappears behind the trees.

"Come on everybody,"
says Mr Baskerville.
"Up to my flat. We'll
see it from there."

Everybody goes up to Mr Baskerville's flat at the top of Skyrise Court to watch the light. It dances around the sky and then as suddenly as it came, it disappears.

The twins are very sad that the light in the sky has gone. "It was fun," they say. "Never mind," says Mr Baskerville. "Now we're all here, we can have a party!"

William blows up some balloons and Hugo makes some sandwiches. "It's not often that we're all together in the same place," says William. "This really is a Pigeon Street party!"

It's quite a party too!
Mr Jupiter joins in the fun
and plays blind man's buff. . .

and Dr Glossop takes
lots of pictures.

"That was a great party," says Mr Jupiter to Mr Baskerville – "thanks to you and that light in the sky. I wonder what it was and where it has gone to now."

The next day, Reg is so busy thinking about that light in the sky, he forgets to dress, and goes to work in his pyjamas.

When Mr Baskerville takes Watson for his walk in Swanlake Park, he is so busy thinking about the light in the sky that he walks into the lake by mistake.

Hugo's mind is on the light in the sky and not on his work. He puts his special dinner for Clara in the washing machine instead of in the oven.

William the window cleaner keeps thinking about that light in the sky. He doesn't notice when Daisy opens the window, and washes her face instead of the glass.

Dr Glossop has put all the photos of the
the light in the sky and of the party into a
special album. "These photos will help us
remember that night," he says. "What a night!"

Mr Jupiter forgets to get up until evening, he's so busy thinking about that strange light in the sky. Then he goes to look for it. "I hope it comes back," he says.